AVISSON YOUNG ADULT SERIES

Freedom's Martyr

*The Story of Jose Rizal,
National Hero of the Philippines*

Suzanne Middendorf Arruda

Avisson Press
Greensboro

ISBN 1-888105-55-0
First edition
Printed in the USA

Library of Congress Cataloging- in- Publication Data

Arruda, Suzanne Middendorf, 1954-
   Freedom's martyr : the story of Jose Rizal, national hero of the
Philippines / Suzanne Middendorf Arruda.
      p. cm. — (Avisson young adult series.)
   Includes bibliographical references and index.
   ISBN 1-888105-55-0 (pbk.)
      1. Rizal, Josâ, 1861-1896—Juvenile literature. 2.
Revolutionaries—Philippines—Biography—Juvenile literature. I. Title. II.
Series.

DS675.8.R5A8 2003
959.9'02'092—dc21
[B]   2003045320

Frontispiece and background cover photos, courtesy of
Ateneo de Municipal University Archives.

Acknowledgements

I would like to thank my husband, Joe, for his support and his very considerable help putting pictures on file for use. Thanks also to Mr. Martin Hester for believing in my capabilities enough to give me another assignment. Special thanks to the archivists at the Ateneo de Manila University for their exceptional help with photographs, especially Ms. Lina Trinidad.

This book is dedicated to all those who work for justice, even if it is just in your home or in your school yard. Treat everyone with respect and dignity.

Contents

CHAPTER 1

CHILDHOOD

The Monkey and the Tortoise: A Tagalog Tale
(translated by Jose Rizal)

The tortoise and the monkey found once a banana tree floating admist the waves of a river. It was a very fine tree, with large green leaves, and with roots just as if it had been pulled off by a storm. They took it ashore.

"Let us divide it," said the tortoise, "and plant each its portion."

Jose Rizal's mother told him to pay attention while she read from *The Children's Friend*, but Jose found the candle flame by which she was reading much more interesting. So his mother found a story about two moths, an old one and a young one.

The old one advised the younger to stay away from flames. They were beautiful, but dangerous. The young moth didn't believe the old one. She was dazzled by the light and flew into the candle anyway. Jose listened with fascination. He later wrote, "My attention was fixed on what happened to the moth . . . I could not blame it. The light had been so beautiful."

Jose grew up with stories as do most children, and most of these stories had morals. The story of the moth and the flame warned children to be cautious of things that seem wonderful because, sometimes, they are dangerous. Another tale from his home in the Philippines, "The Monkey and the Tortoise," taught about greed and treachery. At first, Jose heard and read these stories in Tagalog, one of the many languages native to the Philippines. Jose Rizal Mercado loved his language. In fact, he loved everything about his homeland, the people, their culture, their life under Spanish rule. He wanted the world to know all about the native Filipinos and he would spend his life working to help them.

Jose Protacio Rizal Mercado y Alonso Realonda grew up in a very large family. He was born June 19, 1861, the seventh child of Francisco

Mercado and his wife Teodora Alonso. There would be four more children and plenty of love for everyone. At this time, the Philippine Islands were controlled by Spain, but Jose's family was not Spanish. They were *Indios,* the native people. Jose's family was Malay, very educated and prosperous. Francisco, descended from merchants and a town mayor, leased a lot of land, and ran a sugar plantation. His wife, Teodora, kept a successful shop in the front of the first floor and sold cured hams, jellies, and ran a small rice mill. They lived in a large stone and wood house in the village of Calamba on the island of Luzon.

This town sat between Mount Makiling and Laguna de Bay where waves brushed the sands. Sunshine, bamboo groves, and lovely scenery blessed it, and Jose loved it almost as much as his family. He grew up wandering through the orchard with his *yaya,* or nursemaid. His father built a play hut of nipa palm in the orchard for him. Family was important, and it was the loss of a younger sister, Concepcion, when Jose was four that caused him his first tears.

Jose had only one brother, Paciano, who was

ten years older. Paciano felt Jose had special talents and devoted himself to his care. He taught Jose to swim, ride a pony named Alipato, fly a kite, and to fence. He oversaw Jose's education away from home and provided him with both money and advice in the years beyond.

Jose's parents believed in the value of a good education for all of their children. When Jose was three, his mother started teaching him his alphabet. At first, he read only his native Tagalog, but later his mother taught him to read in Spanish. Not long after, his father hired a former schoolmate to teach Jose the basics of Latin and writing. Even though Spanish was the language of the rulers, Jose didn't ignore his native Tagalog. In fact, Jose wrote his first poem, "Sa Aking Mga Kabata" ("Love of One's Language") when he was eight.

Jose grew up with art, music, and poetry. He kept art supplies such as clay and wax in his play hut in the orchard and worked at sculpting. One day, his older sisters found his work and laughed at him. His sister Narcisa remembered his response. He told them to go ahead and laugh at him now, but people would make statues of him when he died. It was a typical childhood boast, but it would come true.

In 1870 when Jose was nine, his Latin tutor had died, so Jose's father sent him to board with an aunt and attend school in his father's hometown of Binan. This teacher often yelled "Stand up, stupid" to his students and believed in whipping children often. Jose's first day at school was anything but peaceful. His teacher, Justiniano Aquino Cruz, asked him, "Do you know Spanish?" Jose answered, "A little, sir." "Do you know Latin?" Again he answered modestly, "A little, sir."

The teacher's son, Pedro, thought those answers were funny and made fun of the new student. Even though Jose was younger and smaller, he challenged the boy that very afternoon. They fought. "I know not by what chance I licked him, bending him down over some school benches. Then I let him go, leaving him quite mortified. He asked for a return bout, but I refused because the teacher had awakened and I was afraid of being punished. After this I became notorious among my classmates, maybe because of my smallness."

Jose's mother and first tutor had taught him well, so he quickly advanced past many of the older boys. Many of them responded with jealousy and told tales on him to the teacher. This resulted in Jose's being whipped almost every day. Jose resented this unfair, humiliating treatment, but his father wanted him to learn, so he obeyed and took the punishments. Jose learned more than Latin. He learned about injustice and the need for dignity. It would not be his last lesson in either.

Jose also studied art in Binan. His days became very full, but he developed a system of managing every hour and stuck to his schedule. He heard Mass at four in the morning, ate a breakfast of rice and sardines, went to class till 10:00, then returned to his Aunt's house to eat and study some more. At 2:30 he returned to class until 5:00. Then came drawing lessons, a supper of rice and dried fish followed by prayers. Finally there was time for play with his cousins and friends in the moonlight.

In December 1870, Jose received a letter from his eldest sister, Saturnina, telling him that a steamship would take him home again. He collected some river pebbles for souvenirs and prepared to go home. "It is impossible to describe my happiness when I saw the servant who was waiting for us in the carriage. I jumped into it and found myself happy again in my home with the love of my family."

His parents planned to send him to Manila to continue his education, but several terrible events happened one after the other. Jose's mother was arrested and forced to walk nearly 50 kilometers (about 31 miles) to prison. To understand why, it is important to go back many years.

Villages like Calamba were simple. The town hall of Calamba was a sugar shed, and the streets were unpaved. There were no hotels, though the townspeople often opened their homes to travelers. Francisco Mercado Rizal lived in one of the few homes built of stone. He often received visiting Spanish dignitaries in his own home. One frequent visitor was an lieutenant of the local civil guard who also frequently asked for food for his horse.

Years earlier, however, Francisco was not able to offer the officer fodder for his horse. He had none for his own animals and so had none to give. This offended the officer. The civil guard was supposed to protect the citizens, but often they terrorized the *Indios* instead. Now, nearly a decade later in 1871, this same officer conspired with a woman to avenge the insult and have Teodora Alonso arrested for attempted murder.

The woman he conspired with was married to Jose Alberto, a relative of Teodora's. While Jose Alberto was in Spain on business, the wife left him and abandoned her children. It took Jose Alberto a long time to find her, and he planned to leave his unfaithful wife. But Teodora convinced him to be forgiving and to take her back. It seems the woman did not want to go back, and she resented Teodora's 'help.' So she claimed her husband tried to poison her, and named Teodora as his accomplice.

The accusation was clearly false, but the mayor, Antonio Vivencio del Rosario, also felt he had been offended in the past when he had visited the family as a friend. He felt that Francisco had not paid enough respect for his rank. So, he did nothing to help poor Teodora. Jose Rizal wrote many years later, "The mayor . . . treated my mother with . . . brutality, afterward forcing her to admit what they wanted her to admit, promising that she would be set free and reunited with her children if she said what they wanted her to say." It was a trick, however. She was not acquitted until two and a half years later.

As if the unjust arrest of his mother was not enough, events conspired to put another family member at risk. In February 1872, three Filipino priests were singled out and executed for treason after a rebellion at the Kabite navy yard. The Lieutenant General had done several things to anger the native peoples. He didn't allow the opening of new trade schools, he removed many Filipinos from administrative offices, and he gave away all the non-commissioned officer positions to Spaniards. Workers in the Kabite navy yard had been exempt from paying taxes and from going into forced labor. The Lieutenant General abolished that privilege, too. On January 20, over 200 Filipinos took over the arsenal and fort. Seven Spanish officers died in the fighting.

Anyone with liberal ideas was arrested, including the three priests. The men were scapegoats, and native Filipinos saw another example of oppression on their own people. Jose's brother, Paciano, was a roommate and friend of one of these men, Father Burgos. Because of this, he was in danger and had to flee from Manila.

By the time Jose was eleven years old, he had witnessed greed and treachery in the way the Spanish officials dealt with his people, including his own family. These terrible events would have driven other young men to hatred. But Jose Rizal was not like other young men. Instead of seeking revenge, he sought out the beautiful ideal of justice.

The two childhood tales are at work here. They were to entwine themselves in Jose's life and his passionate love for his country. Like the tortoise in one fable, his cause of freedom would triumph in the end over the rulers who wanted everything for themselves and nothing for the native people. But every cause has a price, and like the young moth in the first tale, one day Jose would perish for his beautiful ideal. Jose Rizal would be the moth in the flame and become the country's national hero.

CHAPTER 2

SCHOOL

They cut it in the middle, and the monkey, as the stronger, took for himself the upper part of the tree, thinking that it would grow quicker for it had leaves. The tortoise, as the weaker, had the lower part, that looked ugly, although it had roots.

Jose's mother was still in prison, and he was not yet eleven years old. He wanted to be close to his family. But time can't stand still, and his family wouldn't let him neglect his education. Jose took exams on June 10, 1872 to enter a secondary school in Manila. There were two problems: the school and the Mercado name. Paciano had been a favorite pupil of the recently executed Father Burgos at the University of Santo Tomas. He had spoken out sharply against his arrest and made to leave that school. Instead of entering Santo Tomas, Jose entered the Manila Municipal school, the Ateneo, which was taught by the Jesuit order.

Even in a different school, Paciano decided it

Jose Rizal, in uniform, as a student at the Ateneo Municipal School. (Courtesy Rose Hulman University)

was not safe for his little brother to be in Manila with the first surname, Mercado, after the problems that Paciano had faced. Jose enrolled under his second surname, Rizal. At the age of eleven, he became "a proud Ateneista wearing the school uniform: white coat, striped shirt, black tie, and cream-colored hempen trousers."

His course of studies took six years to complete and included Spanish, Latin, Greek, French, world geography and history, Spanish history, mathematics, mineralogy, physics, botany, and zoology, as well as poetry, rhetoric, and philosophy. To stimulate competition, Jose's class was divided into two groups; the Romans and the Carthaginians. Each group was headed by an 'emperor' which was the top boy. In one month's time, Jose rose to be emperor of his group, the Carthaginians. Jose surprised his mother in prison with a medal for excellent work his first year.

Jose was still small. Because the older boys sometimes picked on, or hazed, the younger, smaller boys, Jose's family boarded him with a family friend, Tandang Titay, a woman who owed them some money. One day, Francisco Mercado dropped by to visit and saw his son playing a card game called *pangginge* with Tandang Titay and other old ladies. What was worse, Tandang Titay was making Jose gamble to win money for herself, since he had such skill. Jose's father was furious. The next year, Jose stayed with a widow lady, Papay del Ampuero.

During Jose's second year, his mother was released from prison, and Jose discovered the wonders of novels. One of his favorites was *The Count of Monte Cristo* by Alexander Dumas. In his third year, Jose didn't perform very well in school. The boarding house was too noisy with students practicing sword play, violin, and piano while others gambled noisily. He only won one prize, for Latin, so despite his small stature, his family decided to board Jose at the school for his fourth year.

Jose was often hazed by the larger boys. Each time, he responded not by fighting back, but by bowing and saying "thank you so much, gentlemen." It didn't take long for the other students to respect this young man. Jose joined several school societies, went to the head of his class, and won five medals. Yet he noticed a distinct inequality in school between the *Indios* and the Spanish students. While some people claimed that Spanish students were simply smarter, Jose reasoned that because the school was taught in Spanish, that made it easier for the Spanish youths; it was their native language, but it was a foreign tongue to the *Indios.*

Jose worked to develop himself in many areas. He practiced fencing to improve himself physically. He also developed his love for poetry. Before he graduated, he wrote an on-the-spot poem titled "Felicitacion" as a birthday tribute for his brother-in-law. A visiting priest, Fr. Leoncio Lopez, didn't believe that such a young boy could write such a splendid poem in that short a time. This hurt Jose's feelings. But when Fr. Lopez saw some of Jose's other writings, he apologized for his mistake to Jose and congratulated him on his talent. The two became close friends. Later in life, Jose would put Fr. Lopez in his second book *El Filibusterismo* as the kind Fr. Florentino.

Jose also practiced sculpting. There is a humorous story handed down in Jose's family concerning one sculpture. It seems that fourteen-year-old Jose was carving a bust of his father, but without his father sitting for it. Perhaps it was to be a surprise. One day, Francisco Mercado, noticed Jose working on the bust, and began to give his own advice on how to proceed. He felt that the eyebrows were too thick, and the chin stuck out too much.

Jose left the statue and ran an errand. When he returned, he discovered that his father had tried to improve upon his work and did some carving himself. Unfortunately, Don Francisco only succeeded in shaving off an eyebrow and removing the nose. The bust remained unfinished but became a family treasure until it was destroyed during the liberation of Manila in 1945.

Jose was never a dull student. He enjoyed the company of other young people including the local young ladies. At the age of fifteen, he first set eyes on pretty Segunda Katigbak, the sister of his friend Mariano Katigbak. As Jose later wrote, "she was not the most beautiful girl I had ever seen, but I have never seen one more alluring and enchanting."

Jose lived in a more formal time, so the first meeting was limited to bows, glances, and blushes.

Jose standing with his palette and canvas. Twice he won top school art awards. (Ateneo de Manila Universidad Archives)

23

Segunda was a student at Colegio de la Concordia where Jose's own sister Olimpia was enrolled. Jose and Mariano visited their sisters frequently. Now the relationship entered the "verbal fencing" stage. She would ask something like, "Do you have a sweetheart?" and he would counter with "Who would ever notice me?" She made an artificial white rose and gave it to Jose. He in turn gave her a crayon sketch of herself that he'd drawn. Jose wrote, "We loved each other without having declared it clearly, except with our glances."

Segunda was already promised by her parents to a kinsman, and the wedding was set for December. She said she was not interested in the wedding. She wanted to remain at the college and study, but Segunda had to obey her parents' wishes. Their romance was doomed. One December day in Calamba, Jose saw her carriage pass by. She waved, he tipped his hat. Segunda was gone from his life.

Jose graduated with honors as a Bachelor of Arts from the Ateneo in 1877. He needed a career choice. His brother, Paciano, was the gentleman farmer caring for the family's estate. Jose considered law as well as farming, but his mother's failing sight finally made him choose a career in medicine. He enrolled at the Dominican University of Santo Tomas and studied a medical course including anatomy, dissection, physiology, hygiene, and pathology. At the same time, he took other courses leading to a degree of surveyor at the Ateneo which he passed when he was seventeen. Still, his mind drifted towards literature.

Many of the novels written at that time concerned injustices. He read Victor Hugo's *Les Miserables,* and it left a great impression on him. In 1879, the Liceo Literario-Artistico sponsored a poetry contest. Jose, then eighteen, submitted "A la juventud Filipina" (an ode to Philippine Youth). He won the prize, a silver pen, for his work. He won something else less desirable, the suspicion of the conservative people. They wondered if there was a hint of rebellion in his poem. He entered a play, *El consejo de los diosos,* under a pseudonym. Again he won the prize, a ring. But the cheers when his play was announced turned to ridicule when the Spanish audience saw that the winner was an *Indio.*

"With intensity had I entered the literary tournament in which unfortunately I won. I heard the sound of applause, sincere and enthusiastic, but on disclosing myself, the applause turned into mockery and insult. Prejudice won over justice."

This was not Jose's only incident with prejudice during those years. One dark, moonless evening in his hometown of Calamba, Jose neglected to remove his hat and salute a lieutenant of the Guardia Civil, the guard that was supposed to protect the citizens. The officer responded by whipping Jose on the street, throwing him in jail, and threatening him with deportation. Jose complained to the authorities and was laughed at for his trouble. Soon after, he received threats. Jose responded not with violence, but by doctoring the poor of Calamba in his third year of medicial school. In fact, his education taught him more than medicine. It taught him how to be a patriot.

Jose later wrote, "At the university I learned more of the injustices of men, of the partiality that disregards worth. I learned of privileges and laws of preference and orders. . . .Very early I had learned to obey; mine was not to reason why. . . . Very early, too, I learned to bow down to authority, to swallow in silence tears of anger and chagrin. Some professors, instead of teaching, would launch on tirades against the race, the country, while we young people silently accepted what we could not fight against. And we trembled, frightened."

Jose believed that the problem of inequality could be solved through education. He believed it would make Filipinos more cultured and better able to challenge Spain to a better rule. His battle cry became, "Education will bring freedom."

Paciano worried about his little brother. He knew about, and sympathized with, Jose's activism. Yet he also knew that violence sometimes erupted. He wanted a calming influence on Jose. According to family stories, Paciano played matchmaker and re-introduced Jose to a cousin and childhood playmate, Leonor Rivera, who now lived in Manila. Leonor was only thirteen, but already she was considered an accomplished young lady. She sang, played the piano, shared Jose's interest in art and books, and became his sweetheart.

Leonor's mother did not approve and the girl was sent away to Concordia for school. Jose and Leonor wrote using their own coded words. Leonor even signed her letters 'Taimis' to avoid her

mother's censorship. The two considered themselves engaged.

According to other accounts handed down in
Jose's family, the brothers had made a secret pact,
a pact they only revealed to their sister, Narcisa,
who later passed on the story so it would not be
lost. Both the brothers wanted to serve their
motherland, but both realized their duty to their
family as well. It was decided that Paciano would
stay and run the family estate. Jose, not encumbered
by other obligations, would dedicate himself to
exposing the troubles of their nation to the world.
His grandniece, Asuncion Lopez Bantug, who
learned the secret from her grandmother Narcisa,
later described their secret mission as one that
would show the true conditions in the Philippines
and bring about reform. The brothers also decided
that only one of them would marry. It was never
clear which one of the brothers that was supposed
to be.

Paciano had formerly encouraged Jose to see
Leonor. Now he wanted Jose to travel. Jose, too,
was unhappy with the Dominican friars' treatment
of native students at Santo Tomas. He wanted to

study elsewhere and see what life was like in other countries. Both brothers knew that their parents would object to Jose going away, so Jose's departure was kept a secret from everyone except Leonor's father, Antonio Rivera. In 1882, after completing his fourth year in medicine, Jose got a passport under the name Jose Mercado. Ironically, his real name was now being used as a pseudonym. Paciano purchased a first-class ticket for his brother.

Jose Rizal left the Philippines, but only in body. His soul belonged to his native country, and he intended to introduce his real homeland to the world.

CHAPTER 3
THE WORLD

After some days, they met. "Hello, Mr. Monkey," said the tortoise, "how are you getting on with your banana tree?" "Alas," said the monkey, "it has been dead a long time. And yours, Miss Tortoise?" "Very nice indeed, with leaves and fruits. I cannot climb up to gather them."

"Never mind," said the monkey, "I will climb up and pick them for you." "Do, Mr. Monkey," replied the tortoise gratefully.

J ose was gone. What all the family thought was a short trip to Manila on May 3, 1882 turned out to be a long voyage to Spain. No one knew when he would return. Jose's uncle, Antonio Rivera, had the unpleasant job of breaking the news to Jose's parents. He wrote:

"Resign yourself therefore to your son's decision, which after all is not wrong . . . You should consider yourself lucky since heaven has given you a sensible and diligent son . . . the envy of other parents."

Jose's parents did not quite see it that way. They grieved over their loss. Leonor, too, had been kept in the dark. She developed insomnia and became very thin. It hurt that her sweetheart would not even say goodbye to her. Jose left letters for them and apologized for his behavior. To his parents and sisters he wrote:

"I know that the great love you have for me would have made my departure impossible, or at least most painful, and so I had to use unusual means . . . But one has to resign oneself to acting as one can and not as one might wish. What would happen if I lived by your side? I would have lived happily, peacefully . . . but later on? Having lived in inactivity and softness, I would have done nothing worthwhile. . . I, too, have a mission to fulfill, a life alleviating the suffering of my fellow men."

He also left behind a love poem for Leonor Rivera:

Goodbye, Leonor, goodbye! I take my
leave,
    leaving behind with you my lover's heart!

Goodbye, Leonor: from here I now depart.
O melancholy absence! Ah, what pain!

Jose was the only *Indio* on the voyage and he listened to the Spaniards speak badly of his country. After changing ships in Singapore, he discovered his fellow passengers spoke English, French, Dutch, Malay, and Siamese. Jose decided to learn as many languages as possible, but managed to communicate well enough using sign language.

His journey took him from Singapore to Port Said, Egypt, then on to Marseilles. Finally, on June 16, 1882, he arrived by train in Barcelona, Spain. Very soon after his arrival, he began his mission. He wrote an essay, "El Amor Patrio" (Love of Country). In it he urged his fellow Filipinos to unite in "ways other than that of fanaticism, destruction, and cruelty." He sent it to the *Diariong Tagalog*, a newspaper in Manila.

Three months later, Jose went to Madrid and enrolled at the Universidad Central. The contrast between Spain and the Philippines was remarkable. In Spain, people spoke and wrote freely. Yet Spain, with all its power, prohibited free thinking and free press in the Philippines. Only in Spain could Jose write about the problems caused by Spain in his own country.

Paciano sent an allowance every month to his brother, but Jose spent very little of it on food. He went to the theater. He bought books. He read *Uncle Tom's Cabin* and decided that a similar Philippine book was needed. He stretched every minute of his day, to the point of exhaustion. A fellow student told how Jose kept himself from falling asleep while studying at night. He attached a weight to his wrist. Then, if he dozed, the weight dragged his arm into a basin of cold water. The cold shocked him awake again.

Jose wanted to show Spain that an *Indio* could be every bit as educated as a Spaniard. However, he was disappointed in his fellow Filipino students. Many had little interest in their studies and none at all in patriotism. But Jose only doubled his own efforts. In 1884, Juan Luna and Felix Resurreccion Hidalgo, two *Indios*, beat all the other painters at an art competition. Jose took the opportunity to speak at a banquet in their honor. He criticized the conditions at home and urged reforms.

"I hope that Mother Spain, solicitous and heedful of the welfare of her provinces, may soon put into practice the reforms that for a long time she has been considering." These words stirred some of his friends to put aside their gambling and become serious students. The speech somehow was also reprinted in the Philippine newspapers. The reactions were of opposite types. Some people were roused to patriotism. Others became furious. His own family became fearful. Jose's mother went to bed with a nervous illness, and his father announced that he wouldn't let his son come home.

Perhaps Jose also understood that his path was leading him into danger. In his diary, he recorded a dream that he had on the night of December 30, 1882. He dreamt that he was playing the role of a dying actor on stage. In his dream, he felt his eyesight dim and felt the darkness of death surround him.

Jose finished his studies and received his licentiate in medicine and a degree in philosophy and letters that June. Unfortunately, he couldn't afford the diploma for a while and couldn't practice medicine without it. He had been doing more than

Jose, seated with his leg atop the table, with friends at Juan Luna's studio in Paris. Luna is in the foreground holding a brush and pallet. (Ateneo de Manila Universidad Archives)

studying medicine during those two years in Madrid. His friends, concerned over his hermit-like behavior, entered his rooms one day and found a half-finished manuscript. Jose had begun work on his Philippine novel, his own *Uncle Tom's Cabin* and *Le Miserables* in which he planned to expose the injustices in his country.

With his medical degree in hand, Jose decided to travel and study elsewhere. He decided to specialize in ophthalmology. In 1885 he went to Paris and studied at the eye clinic of Dr. Louis de Wecker. There was a Filipino community in Paris, and Jose finished another section of his novel. In 1886, he went to Germany where he studied at Dr. Otto Becker's eye clinic in Heidelberg. He also learned how to temper his feelings in Germany and rewrote much of his novel. He mastered the German language and traveled throughout the country. Finally, after writing to the famous Malayologist Ferdinand Blumentritt, an anthropologist specializing in the Malay archipelago , Jose got to meet him. The two men became great friends, and Blumentritt encouraged Jose to complete his book.

Jose did finish his work, in the quiet village of Wilhelmsfeld by the lush forest of Odenwald, while he stayed at the home of Pastor Karl Ullmer. Finally, in June, 1886, Jose completed his novel, *Noli Me Tangere*. He was twenty-five years old. Later, Jose explained the title. "Noli me tangere, words taken from the Gospel of St. Luke, mean 'touch me not.' The book contains, then, things that nobody in our country has spoken of until the

A lighter moment in Paris. Jose (at left, wearing turban) attends a party. A lady friend, Nelly Bousted, is at right. (Ateneo de Manila Universidad Archives.)

present. They are so delicate that they cannot be touched by any one."

On one level, the novel reads like many other romances of the time. There is a wealthy hero (Ibarra) who wants to start a town school but is wronged falsely, and a foolish girl (Maria Clara) who believes her love is dead and eventually enters a convent. The usual evil villains try to take advantage of the girl and the hero. The book is full of anger and resentment. What made the book different, and remarkable, were the vivid descriptions of the minor characters. Here is where Jose Rizal made his mark and introduced the world to life in the Philippines.

No one escaped his pen. Not only did the Dominican friars and the Spaniards appear as scheming and wicked, but the Philippine natives were shown as self-serving dreamers always trying to gain the favors of the Spaniards. The poor people only dreamed of dining with knives and forks, while the wealthier tried to pretend they were not *Indios*. Jose painted a vivid but unflattering picture of the Philippine people.

He drew on his own experiences, and inserted

people he knew and loved. His own Leonor Rivera became a model for the character Maria Clara. He also used people he disliked. In some letters to Herr Blumentritt, Jose explained the model for one nasty character. He described Vicente Barrantes, a scholar who wrote of the Philippines, as ignorant and malicious and compared him to a reptile or hippopotamus.

Even his mother's arrest came into his book as he described a similar incident, the arrest of a lady named Sisa. "She kept her eyes on the ground but, strangely enough, stumbled over stones in the road . . . Blindly, incapable of thought, she only wanted to go away and hide herself. She saw a door; there was no sentry before it but she tried to enter; a voice, more imperious still, stopped her. Stumbling she sought the voice, felt a shove at her back, shut her eyes, tottered forward and, her strength suddenly gone, collapsed on the ground, on her knees and then on her haunches, shaken by a tearless soundless weeping."

He called *Noli Me Tangere* "the first impartial and bold book on the life of the Tagalogs. The Filipinos will find in it the history of the last ten years...The government and the friars will probably attack the work, refuting my arguments; but I trust in the God of Truth and in the persons who have seen our suffering at close range."

Writing a book is only the first part of the task. If it is not published and in the hands of readers, it can't do any good. Most commercial books at that time were published in English, French, or German. Very few were printed in Spanish. That meant that Jose needed to publish it himself. He needed money for printing, about 500 pesos for 1000 copies. Paciano couldn't supply it. The family had already had problems with several bad harvests and rising costs. Jose wrote to his brother, "I don't dare ask you for the amount . . . for a book that might produce more pain than happiness. I'll just hope and wait for luck in the lottery."

The lottery did not play out. By the end of 1886, Jose thought about burning the manuscript. A friend of his, Dr. Maximo Viola, found Rizal in very poor lodgings. He had a fever and was malnourished after eating only one meal a day to save money for printing. Dr. Viola offered a loan which Jose accepted. Soon after, Paciano sent 1000 pesos to Jose for his personal expenses "and if there is anything left, for the printing of the book." Paciano also suggested that his brother come home.

CHAPTER 4

TOUCH ME NOT

And so they walked toward to tortoise's house. As soon as the monkey saw the bright yellow fruits hanging between the large green leaves, he climbed up and began munching and gobbling as quick as he could.

Noli Me Tangere went to press in February of 1887, in Berlin. By March, the first copies were in circulation. Rizal gave the first copy to Maximo Viola and sent others to Blumentritt and the Filipinos of the Propaganda Movement in Madrid and Barcelona. The book became an instant hit and many people offered to follow him "to glory or to the abyss!"

Half a world away, the authorities in the Philippines banned the book's entry and described it as "scandalous, anti-patriotic, subversive to public order, and injurious to the Spanish government." Just like the title, the book became something not to be touched. Jose Rizal had already made enemies in 1884 after his patriotic speech at the banquet. Now his name became a household word.

Despite the ban, the books came in. Any copies entering the Philippines had to be smuggled in. Copies were passed around hand to hand, and people speculated about the various characters. Many were given new covers to disguise them. They might look like a history book or an innocent book of poetry. Jose's aunt Concha Leyba took her book and had several copies made from it. She buried these and dug them up one at a time as someone needed a copy.

Her own original book was kept in a *tampipi* (sewing chest). One day, her house was searched by the Guardia Civil looking for copies of the banned book. Doña Leyba's young housemaid sat on the chest and sewed while the soldiers searched. Other people were caught with the book and jailed for having it. The arrests did not surprise Dr. Rizal, though he was not happy with them. Most distressing, however, the people with the least interest were the Filippino people living in Spain. It was as if they no longer cared about their homeland.

The cover of *Noli Me Tangere*, Jose Rizal's first novel. (Courtesy Rose Hulman University)

Jose wanted to come home. He wanted to be with his parents, brother, and sisters. He longed to see his beloved Leonor. Paciano wrote that he had convinced their father to forgive the "prodigal" and let him come home. So, Jose made the long voyage and arrived in Manila on August 5, 1887 and, two days later, he slipped away to Calamba. His arrival was as quiet and secretive as his departure had been. The authorities knew nothing about it, at least not at first.

Twenty-six year old Dr. Rizal set up an eye clinic and treated the people of Calamba. Some paid him in pesos. But others, poorer with no money to spare, paid him with chickens, eggs, pigs, and fruit. Jose saw that many of the young men in his town spent their spare time gambling and drinking. Always wanting to improve his countrymen, he used some of his money to open a gymnasium for them. News of him spread fast. Jose, suspecting that he may have to leave one day, took 7000 pesos that he earned and bought some diamonds. These could be kept as capital for the next trip.

It wasn't long before his fame reached the authorities, which included the relatively liberal Governor-General Terrero. The Governor sent for Jose and spoke with him, and Dr. Rizal gave him a copy of his book. Terrero liked this young man, but he knew that Jose had many enemies. So he advised him to be careful and assigned a personal body guard for him, Lieutenant Jose Taviel de Andrade, a cultured and educated Spanish gentleman. The two young men became "almost good friends" as Dr. Rizal described their relationship. Jose and Paciano spent time together with, of course, the guard. The three men once hiked to the top of Mount Makiling and waved a white flag to show their accomplishment. Later, Jose's enemies would claim that he waved a German flag over the mountain.

And so Dr. Rizal treated his patients, sketched, and translated German books into Tagalog. What he didn't do was to see Leonor. She was with her family in Pangasinan, over 150 kilometers away. Jose wanted to visit her, but his parents forbade it. Why? They feared for his life if he went anywhere but home. Leonor also asked permission to see Jose, and her parents also refused. They, too, feared for their daughter if she was too closely involved with Jose. Jose and Leonor both were raised with the importance of honoring their parents' wishes. They wouldn't disobey even though it cost them their personal happiness. Jose later wrote, "I should, and could, have gone to Pangasinan; I had a formal engagement; and this was one of my greatest longings for years. Despite the fact that I had nourished this great desire, the opposition of my parents was enough to make me sacrifice all my feelings."

Even though he was busy with his practice, Jose had not given up his project to bring reform to the Philippines. Conditions there were unique and troubling. They were also getting worse. To understand them, it is important to examine some of the history of the islands.

Over a hundred years before Jose's time, the Jesuit order been given land in Calamba. Later in the 18th century, most of the land belonged to independent families. They paid the Jesuits a small fee for irrigation rights. In 1768, the Jesuits were expelled from the Philippines and the Spanish government took over the irrigation lease. This lease passed by auction into the hands of one man who lost it later when he fell into debt. He gave the lease to the Dominican friars.

In 1869, Pope Pius IX commanded the Dominicans and the other religious in Spain to give up their property holdings. The religious in other countries obeyed and followed the order, but not the Dominicans in the Philippines. Instead, they gathered more land and created an estate, or Hacienda. They collected rentals on more than irrigation rights. Their Hacienda grew and swallowed up land owned by independent farmers including Francisco Mercado.

Not only did their land grow, the rents grew as well. Often they gave no receipts, and so the farmer had no proof of payment. The Dominican Haciendas in the Philippines were not always filled with the same good, religious men of other Catholic orders in other places. Many of these men wanted power instead. Often they were assisted by dishonest men in the Guardia Civil, such as the one who had Theodora Alonso arrested years before. They became like the monkey in the fable. The Hacienda and many of the civil authorities took all that was good for themselves and left nothing for those who nurtured the land.

While Jose was at home, the government sent around a questionnaire to the citizens concerning these rentals. Dr. Rizal became involved and interviewed the older citizens. A hearing was held, testimony was read, and people signed the papers to show the recorded testimony was correct. The Dominican Hacienda reacted badly. They threatened to evict all the citizens of Calamba. Jose, himself, was labeled as a *filibustero*, or rebel. People accused him of being a German spy. Others said he practiced witchcraft. Threats were made on his life. Even Governor-General Terrero suggested that Jose should leave the country before he was killed.

It was difficult for Dr. Rizal to stay quietly at home. He had spent so much time in Europe that the hot, humid climate of his homeland now felt oppressive. His family was nervous for his safety, and his sister Olimpia Ubaldo had died in childbirth. Dr. Rizal was ready to leave, but he wanted to marry Leonor first. He talked to his sister Narcisa and to his brother Paciano. Jose said he would leave

Leonor with Narcisa after they married. Narcisa was willing to care for Leonor, but Paciano argued that it was a selfish idea. He said that Leonor would probably suffer more as the wife of Jose Rizal and she wouldn't even have the happiness of having him with her. So Jose sadly left his home without ever having seen his sweetheart. He wrote, "My family would not let me eat outside the house for fear someone would poison me. Enemies burned my books . . . I left my country to give peace to my relatives."

CHAPTER 5
A SECOND TRIP ABROAD

"But give me some, too," said the tortoise, seeing that the monkey did not take the slightest notice of her. "Not even a bit of the skin, if it is eatable," rejoined the monkey, both his cheeks crammed with bananas.

On February 3, 1888, Jose Rizal left on a ship for Hong Kong. He then traveled to Japan, and on to California. Jose was disturbed by the racial prejudice against "Negroes and Orientals" in San Francisco, so much so that he spent very little time in the United States. He traveled rapidly across the country to New York where he received a warning that "a hidden hand may put an end to your life." So he left for London with a new idea. He wanted to disprove the idea that the people of the Philippines had no culture before the Spaniards came. He wanted to meet Dr. Reinhold Rost, a Malayologist, and study his works.

Jose succeeded in his goal. Not only did he meet Dr. Rost, but he discovered wonderful documents in the British Museum. They described a hard-working civilization long before Spain arrived to rule. Jose found documentation of weaving, farming, naval construction, mining, and pearl-fishing. His ancestors were hardly the lazy people that some Spaniards claimed. Rizal copied one of these rare books, Antonio de Morga's *Sucesos de las Islas Filipinas*, with the idea of annotating it and have it reprinted. The author, de Morga, had been an acting Governor at the beginning of Spanish colonization. His testimony would certainly prove to the current Spaniards that the *Indios* deserved respect.

Jose wrote, "I thought it necessary to invoke the testimony of an illustrious Spaniard who controlled the destiny of the Philippines in the beginning of her new era and witnessed the last moments of our old nationality . . . If the book succeeds in awakening in you a consciousness of your past, long erased from memory, then I shall not have worked in vain." The book was published in Paris in 1890. Jose's Austrian friend, Blumentritt, wrote the preface. But the book was not entirely a success. The average person found it too academic to understand, and the scholars thought there was too much bias in it.

Events in the Philippines interrupted his studies in London. In 1889, the more liberal-minded Governor-General Terrero was replaced by Valeriano Weyler. The Hacienda issue was decided in favor of the Dominicans. The people of Calamba protested. Some were arrested, and the mayor brought out the militia. Because of Paciano and Jose's work, their family was in danger. Jose left London for Paris to be closer to news of home.

There was a new journal, *La Solidaridad*, written in Paris by Filipinos away from their home. Dr. Rizal wrote articles for the journal to expose the problems of colonialism. To avoid more problems for his family, he used pen names such as Laong-Laan (Long Ready) and Dimas-Alang (Touch me not) for his articles. In one article, *Filipinas dentro de cien anos*, he predicted that the United States would become interested in the Philippines.

He was also inspired to form a new organization for the Paris Filipinos when he saw a

Buffalo Bill Wild West show at the Paris Exposition. The French cheered the American Indians and shouted "Indians, brave!" Jose decided to make a play on the words and formed *Indios Bravos*. "Indios' was usually used as an insult. Jose hoped the club would turn the name into a "badge of honor."

At the end of 1889, Paciano sent a warning to his brother. He cautioned Jose not to send his letters directly to them because they were intercepted. Paciano urged his younger brother to send them instead to a Senor Basa in Hong Kong.

The years of 1889 and 1890 were terrible for the Mercado family. One brother-in-law, Manuel Hidalgo, was banished. Another, Mariano Herbosa, died but was refused burial in the cemetery. They were constantly harassed. Rumors of rebellions, and police raids slipped out of the Philippines.

These events stirred Dr. Rizal to once again bring the story of the Philippines to the world. He moved to Brussels and started work on a second novel, *El Filibusterismo*. By August, 1890, he finished the first draft of his manuscript. He moved again to Madrid to help appeal his family's legal battles and there, in the fall of 1890, he heard of his family's disaster.

There is a family tradition that the Mercados were ruined because of a turkey. Francisco Mercado raised many turkeys and he always gave a couple of birds to the representative agent of the Dominican Hacienda. Unfortunately, a disease killed most of his flock. The few remaining birds were needed for breeding to rebuilt the flock. There were none to give away.

Rather than understand this, the agent became offended. So the rent was doubled. Jose's father, a peaceful man, paid it. The rent was doubled again. This time, he refused to pay it and he was given a mere twelve hours to leave his property. Twelve hours to pack up a life is not enough. The family could only take their jewelry and the family silver. All the furniture, the house, the barn, and the animals was taken by the Hacienda — all for one turkey and 24 pesos.

Narcisa took her parents into her own home, and the family protested the eviction in court. But it didn't really matter what the court decided. Governor-General Weyler put the entire town of

Calamba under Martial Law and sent in artillery to enforce it. Over 300 families were evicted in the year between March 1890 and March 1891. Homes were burned to ashes. Forty citizens were deported, including Paciano. Entire families faced starvation. Adding to the cruelty was the fact that most of the evictions happened on the day of the town's annual fiesta.

Dr. Jose Rizal wrote in *La Solidaridad*, "We do not seek the expulsion of the friars; we are far from doing to them what civilized Europe and even Spain did: shedding their blood and burning their convents. Our country is more hospitable; and though the friars, with all their policy of hate and oppression, apparently wish to erase from our memory all they once did for us, we shall not forget . . . we shall always be grateful. We only lament to see them taking the place of the executioners."

The Philippine people living in Madrid became more violent over the news from home. Rizal was opposed to this. Even *La Solidaridad*, a paper that was meant to unite the people, caused conflict. M.H. del Pilar became the new editor. He favored the complete liberation of the Malay people from

Spain. He and Jose disagreed; there arose the question as to who was the actual leader, and Dr. Rizal, never one to accept second place, left the paper.

Dr. Rizal was overwhelmed with worry. He feared for his country and the bloodshed that might begin. He worried about his own family. On top of all this came the news that Leonor Rivera had married Henry Kipping, an English railroad engineer in Dagupan.

Leonor didn't really want to marry Mr. Kipping. She told everyone including Mr. Kipping that she loved Jose. But her own mother pleaded and threatened. She told Leonor that Jose had abandoned her, that he never wrote to her. In reality, Leonor's mother had kept Jose's letters from her. Leonor, trained to obedience, finally gave in. She said, "I'll marry him — but he and you both know whom I really love. Anyway, I won't live very long. I beg only one thing, that never again am I asked to play the piano or to sing." They were married in June, 1891.

When Jose heard the news, he was heart-broken. His friend Blumentritt wrote that he was shocked. Jose wrote back, "You should not be amazed that a Filipina should prefer the name Kipping to that of Rizal. An Englishman is a free man, and I am not. Let this be the last word."

Losing Leonor Rivera might have hurt more because his 'engagement' to her was a bit of hope for a happy future in an otherwise restless lifestyle, and perhaps he really did love her. But Dr. Rizal had already fallen in love with several other girls in his travels including Sei-ko, the daughter of a Japanese samurai, and Tottie Beckett, the daughter of his boarding house owner in London. However deep his heartache, he threw himself deeper into his work.

Rizal saw that the battle for the Philippines could no longer be fought in Madrid or France. He needed to be closer to home. But before he could go, he had to publish his second book. Jose Rizal went to Ghent in the summer of 1891, pawned his jewels, and used the money to print *El Filibusterismo*. Copies were smuggled into the Philippines by way of Hong Kong.

El Filibusterismo means 'the dangerous patriot', a man marked by the reigning government who will probably be hanged. The second novel was a sequel to the first, but was darker and more intense. In the book, Ibarra has returned. He's a wealthy man now and living under the pseudonym Simoun the jeweler. His aim is to use his money to make the local government so corrupt that the people will rebel. He plans to get his love, Maria Clara, back too. Add to this, several young *Indio* intellectuals that want to reform the government so that the Philippines can be peacefully brought into full freedom under Spanish rule. But Maria Clara dies and Ibarra's plan to send a bomb hidden in a lamp into a wedding feast goes awry. Ibarra, seriously wounded, flees to Fr. Florentino's mountain retreat.

On his deathbed, Ibarra asks Fr. Florentino why God denied him his just cause for freedom. Fr. Florentino explains, "because you chose a means that He could not approve." The priest says, "we must win our freedom by deserving it, by improving the mind and enhancing the dignity of the individual, loving what is just, what is good, what is great to the point of dying for it." He explains that a rebellion would only make new problems because, "the slaves of today will be the tyrants of tomorrow."

The reader can almost hear Dr. Rizal's own internal debate. He had wanted Philippine representation in the parliament. He wanted native clergy to have parishes. He wanted trade schools and more modern universities to educate his people. He wanted his people to be able to write and speak freely as people could in Spain. He wanted an end to the Dominican Hacienda rule. He still spoke out against violence, but he seems to have given up on Spain ever granting these reforms. Yet he knew the time was not right for total freedom for his country until they had learned to govern themselves. Education was the solution, not bloodshed.

Jose dedicated his book to Frs. Burgos, Gomez, and Zamora, the three priests executed after the Kabite rebellion: "victims of the evil which I am trying to fight." He wrote of the potential glory for his country in his new book. "Tomorrow we shall be citizens of the Philippines whose destiny will be beautiful because it will be in loving hands. Oh, yes! The future is ours, it is rosy. I see life stirring in these regions, so long dead and lethargic."

Many people today look at Dr. Rizal's life as one dedicated to quiet reform. But after the publication of *El Filibusterismo,* even his fellow Filipinos saw him as a "wild firebrand."

Dr. Rizal, himself, saw that violent consequences would likely follow his actions. In a letter to Mariano Ponce he wrote: "One dies only once and, if one does not die well, a good opportunity is lost which will not come again. . . If one must die, let one die at least in his country, for his country, and in the name of his country."

With those words still ringing in the air, he prepared for the journey home.

CHAPTER 6

A TRAP

The tortoise meditated revenge. She went to the river, picked up some pointed shells, planted them around the banana tree, and hid herself under a coconut shell.

As in the fable, the ruling power in the Philippines took from the *Indios* and left very little. Now the native Filipinos, like the ill-treated tortoise, sought revenge. They plotted revolts. Dr. Jose Rizal knew that these tactics would only drive the rulers to lash back against his people. The ones in power would search out the revolutionaries and punish them. Many others would suffer along with them. He was correct, and once again, Jose's mother was one of the victims.

Late in 1891, the aging Teodora Alonso was arrested in Manila. The charge was "the nefarious crime of not using her real name Teodora Realonda de Rizal." The half-blind lady had always been known as Teodora Alonso, yet she was forced to walk 85 km (53 miles) from Manila to Santa Cruz town in Laguna. Dona Teodora offered to pay her own way by boat but they refused her that luxury. She offered to pay also for the expense of the soldiers. Again, the offer was turned down. The trip took three days. When the governor in Santa Cruz saw the poor woman, he released her immediately.

In the meantime, Paciano and his brother-in-law Silvestre Ubaldo escaped before they were deported further south to Sulu. They made their way back to Manila to gather up Francisco Mercado and Teodora Alonso, only to discover that Dona Teodora had already been arrested. In December of 1891, Paciano took his father and they escaped by steamship to Hong Kong. They were soon joined by Jose's mother and three of his sisters: the widow Lucia, and Josefa and Trinidad, both unmarried.

By this time, Jose had been in Hong Kong for a month and was very relieved to have his parents safe with him. In a letter to Blumentritt he wrote, "My aged mother, blind, is also here to escape the tyranny. . . Imagine an old woman of 64 traveling through mountains and highways with her daughter under the custody of the civil guard! She asked to be allowed to travel by boat, offering to pay for all expenses, including the fare of the soldiers, but the "noble Spanish gentleman" did not permit her! When I learned of these 'gallantry and nobility,' I wrote to the 'noble man,' telling him that his behavior towards women and girls was very unworthy; the savages and the Chinese behave more nobly and humanely."

Some accounts record that Jose operated on his mother's cataracts when he was in Calamba. Family tradition claims that is not true. The cataracts were not "ripe" or ready to be removed then. Dr. Rizal did operate on his mother's right eye in Hong Kong and restored her vision in that eye. The left eye would have to wait a bit longer.

Now that Paciano and Jose were together, they could plan their future mission. Paciano translated the *Noli* into Tagalog while they made plans. Both men believed that a revolution would be disastrous. Both brothers leaned towards the idea of setting up a Philippine colony somewhere else. Jose had learned of the British Protectorate in Borneo. Thinking that it might be a possible place for a colony, he traveled to North Borneo to investigate. The situation looked promising. Jose even went so far as to draw up architectural plans for building a Jesuit-style school. However, he soon learned that the plan could not be officially approved. The Governor-General felt it would be unpatriotic to take away any manpower to "foreign soil." Dr. Rizal spoke with the Spanish consul, who persuaded Jose to return to the Philippines. There were too many rumors of unrest. Perhaps Dr. Rizal could do something to prevent such "useless bloodshed."

Jose was passionate about uniting the Philippine people in an organization that would educate them. He wanted to move them into modern agriculture. He wanted them to develop trade and make enough money to invest in machinery. The idea of founding *La Liga Filipina* in his homeland moved him to return home.

The goals of *La Liga* were for uniting all the Philippine islands into one body, to defend against violence and injustice, to develop education and commerce, and to study and apply reforms. What was not clear to the authorities was: how were these reforms supposed to be made? Others wondered if this was merely a front for an underground government. In any case, the *Liga* was a dangerous undertaking.

Jose's family pleaded with him not to go back. Paciano told him it was a bad idea. Jose had always listened to his older brother, Paciano, but not this time. Jose had started a third novel, set in the 17th century. This novel would show the old Filipino virtues and customs. But people had accused him of hiding behind his books and being cowardly. They claimed that it was easy for him to act brave away from the Philippines. Jose wanted to go back. He wanted to "face the bull at close range."

Dr. Rizal suspected he was being led into a trap, and boldly faced it. He left two letters behind which were not to be opened until after his death. One letter was to his family apologizing for the troubles he had brought them. The other was to his countrymen. In it he wrote, "The step I am about to take is risky without doubt . . . I know that my country's future depends in some way upon me. I want to show those who deny our patriotism that we know how to die for our duty and convictions. I have always loved my unfortunate country.

Whatever my fate, I shall die blessing her and wishing for her the dawn of her redemption."

Jose left Hong Kong in June, 1892 with a pass of safe conduct from the Spanish Consulate and a letter for the Governor-General. With these two documents, he felt relatively safe. Little did Dr. Rizal know that the Spanish Consul sent a cable to the Governor-General as soon as Jose left for Manila. The message supposedly read, "The rat is in the trap." When Jose's boat docked, he was met by customs officers, and many officers from the Guardia Civil.

The officers and soldiers searched his luggage, then escorted him and his sister Lucia to the Hotel de Oriente where he booked a room. He went to the Malacanang Palace at four in the afternoon to meet the Governor-General, but was told he could not be received then. He visited his sisters Narcisa and Saturnina and visited with the crowds of people clamoring to see him. In the evening, he returned to the Palace and met with Governor-General Despujol.

Dr. Rizal and the Governor-General met many times through the week. Jose asked for amnesty for his family, and Despujol finally granted it. In between meetings, Jose traveled about. He tried to travel incognito, but it wasn't possible. If only one person recognized him at first, word quickly spread until he was surrounded by admirers who went so far as to kiss his hands. People invited him into their homes for dinner, only to have their houses searched the next day by the *guardia civil*.

On Sunday July 3rd, 1892, Dr. Rizal met in the home of Teodoro Ongjungco. There he spoke about *La Liga Filipina.* Many militant Filipinos were present, and all of them grew excited about the new society and its goals.

Each time Jose returned from a dinner engagement, he checked in with the Governor-General. Despujol asked Jose if he intended to return to Hong Kong, and Jose said yes. On July 7, 1892, Despujol again asked Dr. Rizal if he intended to go back to Hong Kong. Once again the answer was yes. The Governor-General then accused Jose of breaking his word. He also accused him of treason and of making illegal associations. The final charge was for bringing in "seditious pamphlets" from Hong Kong which made terrible statements against the Dominican friars in the Philippines.

These pamphlets, *Pobros Frailes,* did actually make statements against the friars. However, there was nothing in them about the government. Therefore they could not, by definition, be called "seditious." In addition, Jose denied any knowledge of these pamphlets. But the accusers said they found them in the luggage of Jose's sister Lucia. They were tucked inside a bundle of pillows. Jose said that, if his sister did bring them in, she wouldn't have put them where they would be found. Women, he explained, hid things inside their blouses or in their stockings.

Dr. Rizal's family to this day are not sure if Lucia brought the papers in unwittingly, or if the entire episode was a set-up. Most of them believe that the papers were planted there by the very people who claimed to have found them. After all, why did it take an entire week to discover them? Whatever the truth, the authorities did not believe Jose when he said he had nothing to do with them. They took him to Fort Santiago and held him prisoner.

Dr. Rizal was not treated badly. His room had

three windows, and the food was good. His guard even lent him some books. But Jose was not allowed to speak with anyone except the guard. There was no trial. There was not even a formal filing of charges. Governor-General Despujol simply had Jose Rizal deported because Jose was "the tenacious propagator of ideas against the country and the religious orders."

News of the deportation sparked a variety of protests in other countries such as Germany and London. The news caused something else, the end of the peaceful propagandist movement. When Rizal's deportation was announced, several men including Andres Bonifacio met in secret and organized a revolutionary society, the Katipunan, who were not opposed to taking power by a violent overthrow of the government.

Jose wanted to let his family know what was happening, but he was not allowed any visitors. On July 14, Jose was told to get himself ready to leave. He would be taken at midnight to a steamship. He didn't even know his destination, but he came up with a plan to at least let his sister Narcisa know that he was being sent away that night.

Later that evening, a messenger came to Narcisa's house with a note written on the margin of a newspaper. The note, from Jose, asked for his leather hat box. Narcisa questioned the man. Why would he want his leather hat box? The man answered that he didn't know much except that the prisoner was to travel to some unknown destination and wanted the leather box because it might be useful as a life preserver if there was an emergency. In this clever manner, Jose let his family know two pieces of information. First, he was being deported that night. Second, he was traveling by sea.

That night, at midnight, thirty-one year old Jose Rizal learned his destination. He was being exiled to Dapitan in Mindanao.

CHAPTER 7

INTO EXILE

When the monkey came down, he hurt himself
and began to bleed. After a long search he found
the tortoise.

The government officials found and caught the
man they considered to be the mastermind behind
any threat to Spanish rule in the Philippines. He had
injured them too many times with his words. Even
though Dr. Rizal never spoke for violence, he did
speak for change, and change can be dangerous for
those in power.

Thirty one-year-old Dr. Rizal arrived in
Dapitan, a name which means 'to invite,' on July 17,
1892 in the evening. Dapitan housed a Jesuit
mission, and Jose was told he could stay there if he
took back his statements about the friars in the
Philippines. Jose always had a good relationship
with the Jesuits, they had been some of his first
teachers, but he declined the offer. He chose to stay

with the district commandant, Ricardo Carnicero y Sanchez. The commandant spoke with Dr. Rizal and found his views and desires very reasonable.

Jose urged his family to stay in Hong Kong. He hoped that Paciano, who had returned to Manila to help his sister Narcisa after her husband was deported to Jolo, would take Narcisa to Hong Kong as well. After all, amnesty had been granted to Narcisa's husband, Antonio Lopez. They could all be together where they would be safe.

In the meantime, Jose won some money. He, the commandant, and another Spanish gentleman had shared a lottery ticket and won 20,000 pesos. Jose took his share of the money and used half to purchase an estate by the ocean for himself in Dapitan. The rest he sent to his father. Dr. Rizal built a small house, then a larger square house to live in. He added other buildings as well, began a school for boys, and practiced medicine. He discovered a love for farming. Yet he was not a free man. He had to report to the commandant when he left his farm, and had to return by a certain hour.

His school, originally intended to educate the poor children, grew to include some of his own nephews. He taught them useful subjects including science and English. He hunted with the larger boys. He went on nature collections with the younger ones. To keep the boys physically fit, he taught them to lift weights, box, fence, and wrestle. He had the boys build a swimming pool for themselves and came up with a fun way to collect the needed rocks. Dr. Rizal hung a target for his students to throw rocks at. In no time, they had collected a huge pile of stones to make a dam and create the pool.

Dr. Rizal did not brood over his captivity. He immersed himself in work. He invented a machine to make bricks and built a public fountain, a waterworks, and a sanitary drainage system. He earned money and had lights installed in the town. He planted coconut and banana trees. All he missed was his family. He was willing to stay in Dapitan till he died if only they would come and live there with him. Eventually, his mother was allowed to come to him. She and three of Jose's sisters including Narcisa arrived in August, 1893. Along with the joy of seeing his mother again, came the painful news that Leonor Rivera had died two years after her marriage.

Dr. Rizal described his new life later in a letter to his friend Blumentritt. "I am going to tell you how we live here. I have a square house, another hexagonal, and another octagonal — all made of bamboo, wood, and nipa. In the square one my mother, my sister Trinidad, a nephew, and I live. In the octagonal my boys live — some boys whom I teach arithmetic, Spanish, and English — and now and then a patient who has been operated on. In the hexagonal are my chickens. From my house I hear the murmur of a crystalline rivulet that comes from the high rocks. I see the beach, the sea where I have two small crafts - two canoes or *barotos* as they call them here.

"I have many fruit trees — mangoes, lanzones, guayabanos, baluno, nanka, etc. I have rabbits, dogs, cats, etc. I get up early — at 5:00. I visit my fields, I feed the chickens, I wake up my folks, and start them moving. At 7:30 we take breakfast — tea, pastry, cheese, sweets, etc. Afterwards I treat my poor patients who come to my land. I dress and go to the town in my *baroto*, I treat the people there and I return at 12:00 and take lunch. Afterwards I teach the boys until 4:00 and I spend the afternoon

75

farming. I spend the evening reading and studying."

Part of that studying included foreign languages. Dr. Rizal already spoke English, Spanish, German, French, Italian, Japanese, and Tagalog among others, but each night he memorized five new root words. He also studied the other languages of the Philippine islands including Bisayan, Malay, and Subanun.

Dr. Rizal also continued painting. Fr Vicente Balageuer, a Jesuit priest in Dapitan, asked Jose to paint a backdrop for the main altar of the church. He supplied Jose with some rough sketches of an oil painting of Pontius Pilate's court that hung in Barcelona. The canvas was huge, and Dr. Rizal enlisted the aid of Sister Augustina Montoya and Francisco Almirol to help him. The resulting painting was a prized possession of the Santiago Church in Dapitan until it was destroyed by bombs in the Second World War.

Commandant Carnicero was replaced in time by Commandant Sitges. Since Jose wrote his letters in at least four languages, the commandant gave up censoring his letters. But the authorities did not give up on other methods of spying on Dr. Rizal. On one occasion, a man that Dr. Rizal treated admitted that he was a paid spy. Another time, a man came pretending to be an admirer who was possibly sent to kill Dr. Rizal. Otherwise, events took a more ordinary turn, ordinary at least for Dr. Rizal. He devoted himself to an interest in natural history and collected many different specimens for a wide variety of museums. Several species were named for him, too, including *Rhacophorus rizali,* a frog; *Agoponia rizali,* a beetle; and *Draconi rizali,* a dragonfly.

Jose operated on his mother's cataracts but found her to be a poor patient this time. She needed to heal for at least three days, but disobeyed his orders. She got up, walked around, and removed her bandage. As a result, the wound opened and ruptured the iris. His mother argued that someone had struck her while she slept. Still she didn't follow her son's orders and insisted on trying to read and rubbing her eye. Dr. Rizal confessed in a letter to Manuel T. Hidalgo that he knew why doctors are not supposed to treat their own family. Later his mother returned to the Philippines to take care of her sick husband. All the family was free now, all except Jose.

In February, 1895, a young woman came to Dapitan and entered Dr. Rizal's lonely life. Josephine Bracken, an orphan also known as Josephine Taufer, traveled with George Taufer, her foster-father. Mr. Taufer had serious eye trouble and wanted Dr. Rizal to examine his eyes. Josephine was eighteen years old, and Jose found her very charming. It wasn't long after that Jose sent a letter of introduction to his family stating that he wanted to marry this lady. He asked his family to receive her like they would a daughter.

Jose, in the meantime, had written the Bishop of Cebu for permission to marry her. The permission was denied unless Jose retracted his statements about the friars. Jose wouldn't and, since there were no civil marriages in the Philippines, the two were not able to get married.

Josephine returned to Dapitan when Jose's sister Maria visited him. Maria went back home after several weeks, but Josephine stayed behind. She kept house for him and the two lived together, to the shock of his family.

Statue of a boar carved by Jose Rizal during his exile on Dapitan. (Jose Rizal University)

Jose wrote to his sister Narcisa and asked her to come and stay with them. Though Narcisa was willing to try to help the young woman become accepted by the family, not everyone trusted Josephine. Some members of Jose's family felt she might be a spy. Even Jose wondered why the authorities let her come without any questions. They were usually very strict with his other visitors.

A family story handed down by Narcisa suggests that Jose finally confronted Josephine and asked her if she was a spy. The answer doesn't seem to be related anywhere, only that the question made Miss Bracken cry. In March, 1896, Josephine had a premature baby boy who only survived a few hours. Jose buried his son on his little estate.

Family and friends all urged Jose to escape from Dapitan. Many offered boats or money to assist him. Dr. Rizal would not listen to these ideas. As much as he wanted to be free, he knew that escaping would only make him look guilty of involvement in other plots.

But he did listen to one suggestion from his good friend, Blumentritt, who suggested that Dr. Rizal try to enlist as an army doctor and offer to serve in Cuba. Not only was there a revolution there, but also an epidemic of yellow fever. They needed doctors. Dr. Rizal submitted his application. He also wrote to Governor-General Blanco and asked for his freedom or at least for a trial.

On July 30, 1896, Governor-General Blanco gave permission for Dr. Rizal to work as a doctor in Cuba, assigned to the Corps of Military Hygiene.

His sister Narcisa urged him to take the first steamer to prevent the officials from doubting him. Jose had little available money, so he sold away his belongings and made enough money for himself, Josephine, Narcisa and her daughter, and a few of his students to travel.

To the boys who remained behind, Jose divided his remaining property including the chickens. One piece of property would not be passed on. Dr. Rizal had constructed a little *kiosko,* or hut for quiet meditation. Perhaps it had reminded him too much of a similar hut his own father had built for him as a child. Perhaps it was because his own little son would never play in it. Whatever the reason, his last act was to burn the *kiosko.*

Dr. Rizal's boat to the steamer departed to the sounds of a small brass band playing Chopin's *Marcha Funebre*, the Farewell March. It was the saddest song they knew.

CHAPTER 9

ARRESTED

"You wretched creature, here you are," said he. "You must pay now for your wickedness. You must die. But as I am very generous, I will leave to you the choice of your death."

At every port, people surrounded Dr. Rizal. Some wanted to meet the famous man. Others wanted him to treat them. Dr. Rizal operated on one girl with crossed eyes. He operated on another person's ears. He handed out prescriptions. The news spread at each landing that the famous doctor was in port. Jose didn't mind being busy as long as he was helping people.

His original schedule had him arriving in Manila just in time to catch his next ship, the *Isla de Luzon*. There was not time to stop and visit anyone in Manila. The authorities didn't want any of the revolutionaries, the Katipunan, to contact Dr. Rizal. Jose didn't want any of them contacting him, either.

He didn't want anyone to have any reason to be suspicious of him or his motives. It was a cruel piece of bad luck that caused his ship to dock one day late. He missed the *Isla de Luzon*. The next boat to Europe to join his unit would not leave for a month.

Jose stayed on board his ship. His family came to visit him, and nephews played chess with him. Jose never left the ship. Soon, he was transferred to a cruiser, the *Castilla*, which was docked at Cavite. There he would wait for the next mailboat. Jose requested that he not be allowed any visitors except for his family. To add to his safety, Francisco Mercado and Paciano decided not to visit him. Rumors went wild that members of the Katipunan were going to try to free Dr. Rizal. Possible revolutionaries were spotted near the cruiser in small boats. His boat was kept under close guard.

In August, 1896, Bonifacio's Katipunan Revolution took place. Revolutionaries attacked the Spanish powder magazine at Marikina. Even though Dr. Rizal had never left his boat, nor had anyone other than his mother and sisters visited him, the Spanish living in Manila pointed at Jose Rizal as the leader. They wanted him arrested. Governor-

Josephine Bracken, Jose's companion in exile; he considered her his wife. (Jose Rizal University)

General Blanco knew the allegations were not true. He even wrote to Spain to let the government know that Dr. Rizal was innocent of any involvement in the bloody uprising. Just as the revolt ended, the mailboat arrived.

On September 2, Jose Rizal left the Philippines and Josephine behind, but he took with him many worries. What would happen to his poor countrymen? What would happen to his family? Who would take care of Josephine? Josephine did not get along with Jose's family, so she rented an apartment of her own and paid for it by giving English lessons. The only member of Jose's family that she still saw was Narcisa.

Jose soon had more serious worries. His ship, sailing for Barcelona, had to dock first in Singapore. There, two Filipinos came on board with terrible news. It seemed that Dr. Rizal and another man on board were being charged with participating in the Katipunan uprising. They would be arrested. The two messengers urged Dr. Rizal and the other man, Pedro Roxas, to escape into Singapore. Pedro Roxas and his son did, Dr. Rizal did not.

In Port Said, Egypt, Jose learned more bad news from home. He heard the list of names of several Filipinos that were executed. Again, he stayed on board. He trusted in his innocence and felt that escaping only made him look guilty. On October 3, 1896, the ship reached Barcelona, and Jose was placed under arrest. Governor-General Blanco, acting under pressure from the Spanish in Manila, had given the order.

On October 6, Dr. Rizal walked to Fort Montjuich, under guard by soldiers on horseback. There he was searched and threatened. Eight hours later, he was placed on board a ship bound for the Philippines. Also on board were troops sent to smash any remaining revolution in Dr. Rizal's homeland. Dr. Rizal himself was kept in chains in his cabin and not allowed to cover himself with blankets. The lights were kept on all night for the guard to keep watch on him.

In his personal diary, he wrote, "I believe that what is happening is the best that can happen to me. Always let God's will be done! I feel more calm with regard to my future. This afternoon I have meditated because I had nothing else to do nor could I read. I feel that peace has descended upon me, thank God! Thou art my hope and my consolation! Let your Will be done; I am ready to obey it. Either I will be condemned or absolved. I'm happy and ready."

On November 3, the ship arrived in Manila. Dr. Rizal was immediately sent to Fort Santiago as a prisoner. He sent a drawing in ink of Jesus in the Garden of Gethsemane to his family. Under the drawing he noted that this was "but the first station."

Dr. Rizal was charged formally with rebellion and illegal associations. He was said to be the main organizer of the rebellion and wrote to encourage revolutions. A few documents made up the evidence, none of them very incriminating. They included the statutes for his peaceful *La Liga Filipina*, a hymn he had written for his students in Dapitan, and an essay that he denied writing. Yes, he knew some of the men arrested for the rebellion, but no, he had never conspired with any of them.

Desperate for evidence, the authorities arrested Jose's brother Paciano and tortured him for two days. They whipped him, used thumbscrews and a water torture, and pushed pins under his fingernails to make him admit that his brother was in league with the Katipunan. Paciano held true to his beloved brother and was finally released when he became incapable of speaking at all.

Dr. Rizal's remaining family went into hiding. They scattered themselves so if one were captured, not all would be taken. They suspended baskets out of windows so neighbors could drop food in them for them to eat. Everyone lived in fear that they would be arrested next. After all, Jose's own mother had already been arrested twice in the past.

No matter what happened at a trial, Dr. Rizal could not be executed without the consent of the Governor-General, and Governor-General Blanco was against ordering executions. Rizal's enemies knew this and had Blanco removed and his second in command, Polavieja, placed in charge. Now, nothing could save him.

Jose Rizal had always been against violence. He objected to the revolutionaries using his name to rouse people to rebellion. On December 15, he received permission to write a manifesto urging the revolutionaries to return home. In it he condemned the revolt as "absurd, savage, plotted behind my back, dishonoring us Filipinos, and discrediting those who plead our cause." While the authorities were willing to have this manifesto written, they had no intention of altering their decision about Dr. Rizal's guilt. In the end, they did not even publish it, because it only condemned the violence of the uprising, not the revolt itself. They believed Dr. Rizal secretly approved of the rebellious movement. On December 19, Governor-General Polavieja ordered a trial.

Luis Taviel de Andrade was the younger brother of Jose's friendly bodyguard in 1887. This was the man that Dr. Rizal chose to defend him in court, and the young man did that with great vigor. In fact, his superiors became very displeased with him for trying so hard to defend Dr. Rizal. Jose Rizal, in the meantime, sat quietly with his elbows tied behind him.

The court-martial took place on December 26 at 8 a.m. Josephine Bracken managed to be present in a hall packed with Spaniards. The death penalty was demanded. The defense argued that all prosecution evidence was based on documents written long before the revolt took place and for which Jose had been punished by deportation. Dr. Rizal offered proof that, not only had he not participated or instigated the revolt, he had actually worked to peacefully bring about change. He had never sought to overthrow Spanish rule. He had never tried to escape. All this fell on deaf ears. The decision was made. Jose Rizal received the death sentence and he or his family were ordered to pay one hundred thousand pesos as a fine.

The Governor-General approved the death sentence on December 28. The execution was marked down for 7 a.m.,Wednesday, December 30, 1896. Jose's mother wrote a passionate letter to the Governor-General to spare her son. Respectfully, she declared his innocence. She delivered the letter herself to the palace but was not able to secure her son's reprieve.

Rumors began that the Katipunan were going to break into the fort to release Dr. Rizal. Paciano heard these reports and, in spite of his weakened condition, tracked down the men in charge to advise against their plan. He knew that the soldiers would be waiting for such an attempt. Such a plan would only bring about more death. The death of his dear brother, Jose, was bad enough without having it marked by the death of more people.

CHAPTER 10

INTO THE FLAME

"Shall I pound you in a mortar or shall I throw
you into the water? Which do you prefer?"

"The mortar, the mortar," answered the
tortoise; "I am so afraid of getting drowned."

"O ho!" laughed the monkey; "indeed! You
are afraid of getting drowned! Now I will drown
you." And going to the shore, he slung the tortoise
and threw it into the water.

How glorious to die for such a beautiful cause, that was what a younger Jose thought about the moth. Now he would die for his cause. The story of the moth and the flame has been used many times to portray Dr. Rizal's death for his country. But there was more than the death of one man at stake here. The ruling government want to kill all hopes of change for the *Indios* in the Philippines. They are the monkey in the second fable, and the native *Indios* with their cause of liberty are the tortoise.

With the death of Dr. Rizal, the government hoped to end any rebellious attempts by the Filipinos.

The government had his manifesto decrying violence and they would have his death. It would also certainly help the friar's cause if Dr. Rizal would take back, or retract, his radical ideas of free thinking in religion. According to many people, he did just that, and they have a document to prove it. Handwriting experts claim the signature is authentic.

Others claim the retraction was a forgery. They say that Dr. Rizal couldn't admit to errors if he didn't make any. There was even disagreement in the family. Paciano claimed his brother did not make a retraction. Other friends said that the supposed retraction actually just admitted the basic ideas of the Catholic faith. It did not express any opinions about politics or corruption within the local church. After all, just because the revolution was anti-friar, it doesn't mean that it was anti-faith. So perhaps Jose did sign such a statement after all. It's difficult to know just what goes through a person's mind when they know they are about to die.

Then what actually happened in those last

hours of Dr. Rizal's life? What is fact? He wrote a farewell poem to his family and some last letters of farewell. He asked for a copy of *The Imitation of Christ*. Jose wanted his family to see him one last time, but the officials only let the women come. His mother, and five sisters: Lucia, Josefa, Maria, Narcisa, and Trinidad visited. Narcisa brought her eleven year old son, Leoncio, and Maria brought her little boy, Mauricio. The women came to his cell one at a time. They were not allowed to touch him. Leoncio was told to wait outside.

Jose gave away his few remaining possessions. Narcisa got a wicker chair, his niece Angelica a handkerchief. Mauricio was given a belt with a watch and chain. To Maria he gave a message that he was going to marry his Josephine, something that could only be done by a priest. Perhaps this was a way of telling them that he had given up his free-thinking ideas and taken back the basics of his faith. Jose spoke softly in English to Trinidad. He told her he had something hidden in his shoes and in his alcohol lamp.

As they women left, a guard brought out the lamp, and Narcisa took it for their parents to keep.

She didn't know about the secret because her English was not as good as Trinidad's. When they got home, Trinidad told them about Jose's message. They took the lamp apart and used hairpins to remove a sheet of paper wedged inside. Inside was a poem of 70 lines, 14 stanzas titled "My Last Farewell." He wrote:

I am to die when I see the heavens go vivid,
announcing the day at last behind the dead
night.
If you need color, color to stain that dawn with,
let spill my blood: scatter it in good hour:
and drench in its gold one beam of the newborn
light.

Jose had one more visitor when his family left. Josephine came in the late afternoon. Some stories claim that they were officially married then. Others doubt it because it would mean he did retract his free-thinking ideas on religion. But she and Jose always considered themselves married. He even left her the copy of *The Imitation of Christ* dedicated to 'my dear and unhappy wife, Josephine.'

His farewell letter to his father asked for forgiveness. The one to Blumentritt announced his death. A third letter to his sisters asked them to take care of their parents, to give him a simple headstone, and not have any anniversaries of his death. Finally, his letter to his beloved brother, Paciano, told him how sorry he was to leave his brother with the care of the family. He apologized for all the suffering that Paciano had undergone, but that he died innocent of the crime of rebellion. At five in the morning he married Josephine. They were not permitted to touch.

Dr. Rizal went out to the execution grounds in the morning of December 30, 1896. He wore a black suit with a white shirt and a white tie. A bowler hat sat on his head. His arms were again tied behind him at the elbow. A crowd of Spaniards had gathered to watch.

In the early hours at 6 a.m. Jose walked to the Luneta, a small park named for its crescent moon shape which stood near the sea where the bay curves. The sky was cloudy and the December air was chilly. Spanish and Filipino soldiers formed

The only known image of the execution of Jose Rizal, in Luna Park, Manila. (Ateneo de Manila Universidad Archives)

three sides of a square in the Luneta, leaving the bay side open.

The drum corps began to play but the drum roll was muffled by the black drapes over them used for executions. Soldiers with bayonets marched in leading Dr. Rizal, an officer, and a Jesuit priest. The officer shook hands with Jose. It was Lieutenant Luis Taviel de Andrade, the young man who had tried so hard to defend Dr. Rizal in court.

Dr. Rizal faced the bay. A colonel went to

each of the four corners to shout his order. He proclaimed that anyone who spoke in favor of the criminal would be executed. Only the sound of the bay could be heard after that. The priest blessed Jose, an officer positioned the firing squad, and Dr. Rizal took off his derby hat. It was a difficult task since his arms were still tied. He was allowed to stand for his execution rather than suffer the indignity of kneeling and being shot in the head.

An officer pointed with his sword and signaled the firing squad to take aim. The sword dropped and they fired. Jose Rizal twisted and fell. After a doctor checked for a pulse, a soldier was called forward to give another shot at close range to make certain the prisoner was dead.

Jose was executed on the very date that he had his prophetic dream of death fourteen years earlier.

After the execution, Narcisa sent a coffin to the Luneta to get her brother's body, but no one could find it. The corpse had been removed already. She went to cemetery after cemetery looking to find a freshly dug grave, or someone who would know where her brother was buried. No one knew or, if they did, they didn't tell her. Finally, after a long

search, Narcisa came to the old city cemetery, Paco
Cemetery. No one used it any more, but she saw
several soldiers around a fresh grave. After they left,
Narcisa found the sexton in charge and asked him to
mark the grave with a small slab of marble that she
had. On the small headstone were three letters,
R.P.J. These were Jose's initials in reverse order.
The family feared that anything else might be
removed, or worse yet, cause someone to move the
body. No one had a chance to see what Jose had
hidden in his shoes.

CHAPTER 11
A FREE HOMELAND

But soon the tortoise reappeared swimming and laughing at the deceived artful monkey.

Executing a public hero was a mistake for the colonial masters. Instead of ending any more attempts at change, it only sparked more insurrection.

For two terrible years, the native Filipinos fought Spanish rule. Then events half a world away would change everything. The United States and Spain stumbled into a war that involved Spain's far-flung colonies. On May 1, 1898, a United States fleet under Commodore George Dewey entered Manila Bay and sank an antiquated Spanish armada; this action effectively put the Philippines under U.S. control. The Treaty of Paris formalized the change and began a long association between the islands and the United States. After all the long centuries since Magellan, Spanish rule was over. Dr. Rizal's family used the opportunity to remove his body from the original grave site and rebury it with honor. Whatever had been in the shoes had long since rotted, since Jose had not even been put into a coffin by his executioners.

Not all the Filipinos accepted America's control of their country, and something like a war broke out, contained but savage, against the U.S. by nationalists. This was put down with great force and occasional cruelty. Emilio Aquinaldo, a patriot, led a small force against the U.S. for four years until his capture. Others cautiously tried to accept the new regime as the relationship slowly changed from violence and fighting to one that was mostly benevolent, if paternalistic.

The new rulers insisted on the separation of church and state, which ended the rule of the Dominican friars. By 1907, the Philippine assembly became the first freely-elected legislature in all of Asia. In 1935, the country's status was changed to one of Commonwealth. After three years of Japanese domination during the Second World War, during which time Filipino guerillas fought courageously with the Allied forces, in the summer of 1946, by mutual agreement, the Stars and Stripes were lowered in Manila and the new flag of the Philippines was raised. A new and independent nation inaugurated their first President, Manual A. Roxas. The date was July 4, now a shared Independence Day.

So the dream of Jose Rizal, one of Philippine self-determination and dignity among the other sovereign powers, came true.

What makes a hero? Many people were involved in finally gaining the Philippines' freedom. Why then is Dr. Jose Rizal esteemed as a national hero above all the others? Jose Rizal had longed for his people to be treated equally by Spain. He hoped for fair representation in Spanish Parliament. The actual results went beyond his dreams. His homeland was a nation ruling itself. He taught his people that they were more than just separate islands with different languages, they were all Filipino. The dream of liberty survived, and his country honors him for that.

Statues of Dr. Rizal sprout in Dapitan, in

Manila, and at the Jose Rizal University in Mandaluyong City, Philippines. There are parks named for him and monuments erected to him. His childhood home has been rebuilt and preserved, as are the huts which he built in Dapitan. There are even statues of him in Honolulu, Hawaii and in Wilhelmsfeld, Germany. Dr. Rizal was always a charismatic person, someone with personal charm that drew others to him no matter what their country or language. His legacy still draws people to him and inspires them today.

Selected Bibliography

Bantug, Asuncion Lopez, *Lolo Jose: An Intimate Portrait of Rizal*, Instramuros Administration, Manila, 1982

Chapman, William, *Inside the Philippine Revolution*, W.W. Norton & Company, New York, 1987.

Guerrero, Leon Ma., *The First Filipino, A Biography of Jose Rizal*, The Journal Press, Quezon City, Philippines, 1963.

Montemayor, Teofilo H. "Jose Rizal: A Biographical Sketch," Jose Rizal University website http://www.joserizal.ph/bigraphy.htm.

Palma, Rafael, *The Pride of the Malay Race: Jose Rizal*, translated by Roman Ozaeta, Prentice-Hall, Inc., N.Y., 1949.

Rizal, Jose, *Quotations From Rizal's Writings*, Jose

Rizal National Centennial Commission, Vol X, Manila,1962.

Rizal, Jose, *El Filibusterismo*, (English translation), translated by Leon Maria Guerrero, Indiana University Press, Bloomington, 1962.

Rizal, Jose, *The Monkey and the Tortoise, A Tagalog Tale* (translated from the Tagalog by Jose Rizal).

Rizal, Jose, *Noli Me Tangere* (English translation), translated by Leon Maria Guerrero, Longmans Publishers, London, 1961.

Simons, Lewis, *Worth Dying For*, William Morrow and Company, Inc., New York, 1987.

The Jose Rizal website at Rose-Hulman University is maintained by Dr. de la Cova.
http://www.rose-hulman.edu/%7Edelacova/rizal.htm

Index

About the Author

SUZANNE MIDDENDORF ARRUDA is a former middleschool / high school teacher and is currently an instructor at Pittsburg State University in Kansas. She is a member of the Joplin Writer's Guild, Missouri Writer's Guild, and the Society of Children's Book Writers and Illustrators. She has published one other biography, *From Kansas to Cannibals: The Story of Osa Johnson*, as well as stories and articles in magazines. She lives with her husband, Joe, twin sons Michael and James, a cat named Wooly Bear, and a dysfunctional parakeet, Ozymandias.